THE HISTORY OF THE GREEN BAY PACKERS

THE HISTORY OF THE
GREEN BAY

Published by Creative Education

123 South Broad Street

Mankato, Minnesota 56001

Creative Education is an imprint of The Creative Company.

DESIGN AND PRODUCTION BY **EVANSDAY DESIGN**

Copyright © 2005 Creative Education.

International copyright reserved in all countries.

No part of this book may be reproduced in any form

without written permission from the publisher.

Printed in the United States of America

LIBRARY OF CONGRESS CATALOGING-IN-PUBLICATION DATA

Nichols, John, 1966–

The history of the Green Bay Packers / by John Nichols.

p. cm. — (NFL today)

Summary: Traces the history of the team from its beginnings through 2003.

ISBN 1-58341-297-2

1. Green Bay Packers (Football team)—History—Juvenile literature.

[1. Green Bay Packers (Football team)—History.

2. Football—History.] I. Title. II. Series.

GV956.G7H57 2004

796.332'64'0977561—dc22   2003065105

First edition

9 8 7 6 5 4 3 2 1

COVER PHOTO: running back Ahman Green

PHOTOGRAPHS BY

AP/Wide World Photos, Corbis (Bettmann, Reuters), Getty Images, Icon Sports Media Inc., SportsChrome USA

PACKERS

John Nichols

AT A GLANCE, GREEN BAY, WISCONSIN, SEEMS NO DIFFERENT THAN MANY AMERICAN CITIES. SET IN THE STATE'S NORTHEAST CORNER ON THE SHORES OF LAKE MICHIGAN, IT IS HOME TO 100,000 PEOPLE WHO WORK HARD AND SPEND MUCH OF THEIR FREE TIME ENJOYING THE AREA'S ABUNDANT WATERS AND WOODS. TRULY, GREEN BAY COULD BE JUST ABOUT ANY CITY, EXCEPT FOR ONE THING. LITTLE GREEN BAY IS HOME TO PERHAPS THE MOST FAMOUS FRANCHISE IN THE NATIONAL FOOTBALL LEAGUE (NFL): THE GREEN BAY PACKERS. THE TEAM GOT ITS START IN 1919 AS A FOOTBALL-LOVING COLLECTION OF FACTORY WORKERS AND WAS NAMED THE PACKERS AFTER A MEAT PACKING COMPANY PURCHASED ITS UNIFORMS AND EQUIPMENT. SPORTS FANS IN GREEN BAY AND THROUGHOUT WISCONSIN QUICKLY FELL IN LOVE WITH THE TEAM, AND GAME DAYS IN THIS NORTHERN REGION HAVE BEEN REASON FOR CELEBRATION EVER SINCE.

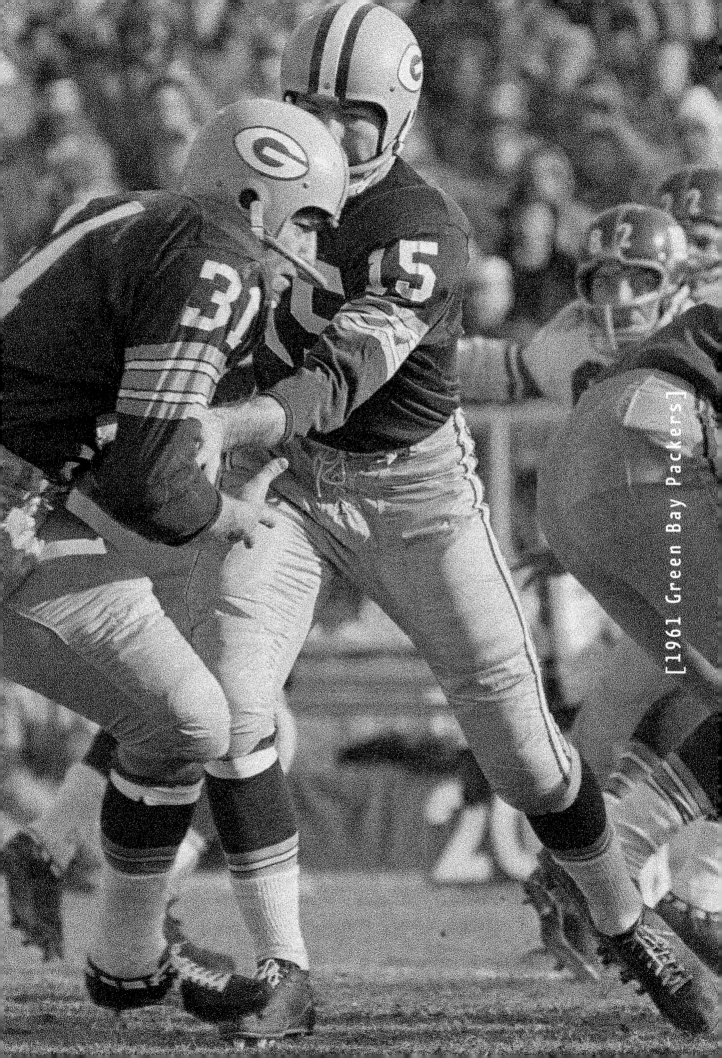

[1961 Green Bay Packers]

ON THE EVENING of August 11, 1919, a group of burly young men gathered in a Green Bay newspaper office. The meeting's organizers, Earl "Curly" Lambeau and George Calhoun, both loved football and wanted to start a team. After finding enough players, the two men got Lambeau's employer, a local meat packing company, to put up $500 to get a team started.

In 1921, the Packers joined the new NFL. The driving force behind the Packers in those early years was Lambeau. During the team's first 11 seasons, he served as both head coach and running back. A smart and disciplined leader, Lambeau is credited with being the first coach to make the forward pass a major part of his offense. "Curly was always ahead of his time," noted running back Johnny "Blood" McNally, a Packers star of that era. "He was always thinking of ways to get an edge."

Despite Lambeau's leadership on the field, the Packers often had difficulty making ends meet. Several times, Lambeau sought financial help to keep the team afloat. Finally, in 1922,

the Packers were bought by a group of local businessmen who formed the Green Bay Football Corporation. It established the Packers as a team completely owned by the citizens of Green Bay, a unique status that continues to this day.

With his money problems solved, Lambeau led the Packers to a 12–0–1 record and their first NFL championship in 1929. The following season, Lambeau retired as a player and concentrated on coaching. Under his direction and behind the great play of offensive tackle Cal Hubbard and quarterback Arnie Herber, Green Bay captured two more NFL titles in 1930 and 1931.

In 1935, Lambeau signed a young receiver from the University of Alabama named Don Hutson. Sure-handed and blazing fast, Hutson was the NFL's first star receiver. During his 11-year career, he caught 99 touchdown passes (an NFL record that stood for 44 years) and led the league in receptions eight seasons. Hutson's brilliant play propelled the Packers to three more NFL championships in 1936, 1939, and 1944.

After the 1945 season, Hutson retired. Without his heroics, the Packers fell from contention. At the end of the 1949 season, Lambeau stepped down as coach, and Green Bay fell into a losing spiral that would last through much of the 1950s.

QUARTERBACK TOBIN ROTE and receiver Billy Howton had some great seasons in the early 1950s, but the Packers struggled. Three different coaches tried to right the ship after Lambeau's departure, and all three failed. In 1958, the once-proud Packers hit rock bottom, going 1–10–1.

Desperate to turn things around, the team then hired a little-known assistant coach from the New York Giants by the name of Vince Lombardi. Lombardi so impressed the hiring committee that he was soon named Green Bay's general manager as well. Assembling his players for the first time in 1959, Lombardi made it clear things were about to change. "Gentlemen, I've never been part of a losing team," he announced, "and I don't intend to start now."

Lombardi's plan to revive the Packers was based on hard work and discipline. He drilled his team on fundamentals and stressed physical conditioning. His hard lessons were not always well-received, but his team responded. "Coach Lombardi challenged us to get better everyday," said Packers running back Paul Hornung. "Sometimes we hated him for it, but he made decent players good, good players great, and great players Hall-of-Famers."

One advantage Lombardi had in rebuilding the Packers was that the team had a core of talented young players already in place. Hornung, running back Jim Taylor, quarterback Bart Starr, linebacker Ray Nitschke, offensive tackle Forrest Gregg, and defensive backs Willie Wood and Herb Adderly would all eventually be enshrined in the Hall of Fame, but it took Lombardi's demanding coaching style to coax greatness out of them.

In 1960, the young Packers reached the NFL championship game against the Philadelphia Eagles but came up short, 17–13. Then, the next two seasons, they stormed to two consecutive NFL titles, drubbing the New York Giants 37–0 in 1961 and 16–7 in 1962. Having celebrated seven NFL championships, Packers fans gave their community a new nickname: "Titletown, U.S.A."

Jim Taylor powered the Packers offense with 1,000 or more rushing yards in five straight seasons

WHILE LOMBARDI WAS the driving force behind the Packers on the sidelines, quarterback Bart Starr was the onfield leader. Starr's cool, calm leadership contrasted sharply with Lombardi's loud, fiery style. But while the two men differed in personality, they shared a dedication to perfect execution. "Sometimes I wondered if Bart wasn't a machine," Packers guard Jerry Kramer once said. "It seemed like he never made a mistake, never showed any pain, and never missed an open receiver."

Starr ran the potent Packers offense like an orchestra conductor, quietly directing his teammates to perform their roles to perfection. With Starr throwing the ball to receiver Carroll Dale and handing it off to Hornung and Taylor, the Packers captured another NFL championship in 1965, defeating the Cleveland Browns 23–12.

Legendary quarterback Bart Starr was selected in the 17th round of the NFL Draft in 1956.

Playing as both a rusher and kicker, Paul Hornung led the NFL in scoring in 1959, 1960, and 1961^

Before the 1966 season, the NFL and a rival league, the American Football League (AFL), decided to merge. The leagues would keep separate schedules until 1970 but agreed to play an AFL-NFL championship game starting in 1966. The Packers captured the 1966 NFL title and met the AFL champion Kansas City Chiefs in what was then called the AFL-NFL World Championship Game. Green Bay whipped the Chiefs 35–10 behind two Starr touchdown passes. Shortly thereafter, the game became known by the name it holds today: Super Bowl I. It seemed fitting that the Packers, who had written so much of the NFL's early championship history, should win the very first Super Bowl.

LOMBARDI'S LAST HURRAH>

BY 1967, GREEN BAY was an aging team, with many of its stars in their 30s. Despite their advanced years, the Packers captured another NFL title, this time defeating the Dallas Cowboys in the championship game—a game remembered as one of the most famous in NFL history.

The game was played at Lambeau Field in Green Bay in such bitterly cold conditions that the contest later became known as the "Ice Bowl." His team trailing 17–14 with 13 seconds left in the game and the Packers on the Cowboys' one-yard line, Starr called timeout. After Lombardi told Starr to go for the winning touchdown instead of the tying field goal, Starr took the snap and burrowed into the end zone for the winning score. "That was a game of guts," said Packers defensive tackle Henry Jordan. "Other teams would have quit in that cold. We didn't."

Two weeks later, Green Bay thrashed the Oakland Raiders in Super Bowl II, 33–14. The lopsided win was historic in several ways. It marked the second time the Packers had won three straight championships, something no other franchise had done even once. The win was also the last for the legendary Lombardi in Green Bay. Exhausted after nine seasons as coach and general manager, Lombardi turned the coaching reins over to his assistant Phil Bengtson.

In 1968, the Packers missed the playoffs. Shortly after the season, Lombardi left town to take over as coach and general manager of the Washington Redskins. Lombardi's comeback would last only one season, however, before he suddenly died of cancer at the age of 57. To honor him, the NFL named the trophy awarded to the Super Bowl champion the Lombardi Trophy.

Such 1960s greats as linebacker Ray Nitschke established a tradition of defensive excellence in Green Bay

LOMBARDI'S DEPARTURE MARKED the end of the Packers dynasty of the 1960s, and Coach Bengston resigned in 1970 after three poor seasons. Throughout the 1970s and '80s, Packers fans enjoyed some great individual performances from such standouts as bruising running back John Brockington, speedy wide receiver James Lofton, and quarterback Don Majkowski, but victories were few. From 1968 to 1991, the Packers posted just five winning seasons.

Sterling Sharpe (pictured) succeeded James Lofton as the Packers' top wide receiver in the late 1980s^

Brett Favre (with ball) was famous for his toughness, starting 208 straight games from 1992 to 2003.

Seeking to revive the franchise, the Packers hired Mike Holmgren as head coach in 1992. Holmgren had been an assistant coach with the powerful San Francisco 49ers and had earned a reputation as one of the top offensive strategists in the game. "Mike was a winner, and his attitude rubbed off on us immediately," said receiver Sterling Sharpe, one of the team's brightest stars of the early 1990s. "He told us we could be good and rebuilt our pride."

Holmgren's rebuilding plan centered around Sharpe, hard-hitting safety LeRoy Butler, and young quarterback Brett Favre. The strong-armed Favre had been acquired by the Packers in a trade with the Atlanta Falcons before the 1992 season. The Falcons thought Favre was too raw and undisciplined, but Holmgren saw a promising player with a gift for pulling great plays out of thin air.

Another key step in the Packers' revival was the signing of defensive end Reggie White before the 1993 season. Standing 6-foot-5 and weighing 300 pounds, White was a giant of a man widely recognized as the best defensive lineman in the game. When he arrived in Green Bay, Packers fans sensed that good things were just around the corner.

Favre and White led Green Bay to playoff appearances in 1993, 1994, and 1995, but the team was thwarted each time by its old rival: the Dallas Cowboys. In 1996, there was no denying the Pack, as Favre threw 39 touchdown passes and led Green Bay all the way to the Super Bowl. Facing the New England Patriots for the title, the Packers rode Favre's two touchdown passes and White's three quarterback sacks to a 35–21 victory. "It's great to bring a championship back to this town," Favre said joyfully. "Our fans deserve this."

The next season, Favre threw 35 touchdown passes to win the NFL's Most Valuable Player award for the third straight year, and the Packers returned to the Super Bowl. Unfortunately, Green Bay came up short this time, losing 31–24 to the Denver Broncos. Following the 1998 season, White retired and Holmgren left town to become coach of the Seattle Seahawks.

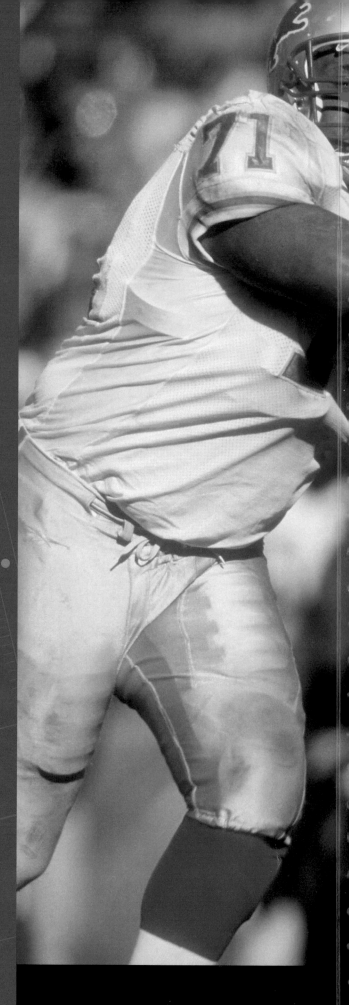

An almost unstoppable force, end Reggie White averaged 11 sacks a season during his Packers career^

THE PACKERS REMAINED a contender through the end of the 1990s and into the 21st century. Favre continued to set one new NFL passing record after another, but perhaps his most impressive record was set in 1999 when he started his 117th consecutive game, breaking the league record for quarterbacks set by the Philadelphia Eagles' Ron Jaworski. "That tells you a lot about Brett," said Packers wide receiver Antonio Freeman. "He is so competitive and tough you can't keep him off the field."

In 2000, the Packers hired Mike Sherman as their new head coach. Sherman knew that the Packers were still a strong team but needed to add some youth to the veteran roster. The new coach began to develop such talented youngsters as explosive running back Ahman Green, wide receiver Donald Driver, defensive tackle Cletidus Hunt, and safety Darren Sharper.

Known for his acrobatic catches, Donald Driver was the latest in a long line of great Packers receivers

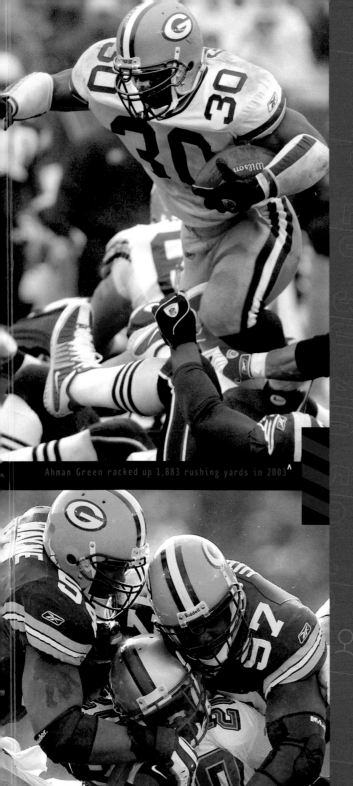

Ahman Green racked up 1,883 rushing yards in 2003^

Cletidus Hunt (right) was a 300-pounder with speed^

The Packers returned to the playoffs in 2001, 2002, and 2003, but fell short of the Super Bowl each year. In 2001, they were knocked out of the postseason by the St. Louis Rams, 45–17. In 2002, they were stunned by the upstart Atlanta Falcons, losing 27–7 at Lambeau Field. And in 2003, they lost a 20–17 heartbreaker to the Philadelphia Eagles. Still, Green Bay players and fans alike believed the best was yet to come. "Don't worry about us," said cornerback Mike McKenzie. "We'll be back."

Although the Packers started small more than 80 years ago, over the decades they have grown into perhaps the NFL's most storied franchise and become a key part of the lives of the people of Green Bay. In a city of barely 100,000 people, the team's 70,000-seat stadium has sold out for every home game since 1960. Today's Packers plan to reward their fans for this amazing support and bring the Lombardi Trophy to Titletown once again.

INDEX>